C000219591

100 Cracking Jokes

The Best from the Valleys

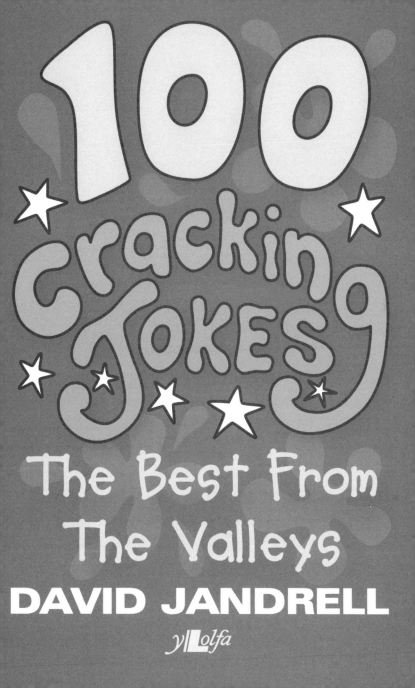

100 Cracking Jokes

The Best From The Valleys

DAVID JANDRELL

y Lolfa

ISBN: 0 86243 871 3
9780862439279

Printed on acid-free and partly recycled paper
and published and bound in Wales by
Y Lolfa Cyf., Talybont, Ceredigion SY24 5AP
e-mail ylolfa@ylolfa.com
website www.ylolfa.com
tel (01970) 832 304
fax 832 782

Not Welsh, Irish, Scots, or English Jokes: just 100 Blinkin' Good 'Uns!

"So, another joke book… what's new?" I hear you say. What's new is that this one contains no Irish, Welsh, Scottish, Racist, sick or sex jokes!

Historically, joke books have been categorised into subject areas, where ethnic stereotypes have been derided in the name of comedy. Some fallacies: the Scots and the Jews are tight, the Irish are thick, the Welsh are besotted with rugby *and* sheep and so on.

There is not a great deal of material with which to vary 'ethnic' jokes that much, as all of them seem to have to contain these so-called 'characteristic traits' – has anyone ever heard a joke about an intelligent Irishman? I don't think it would work, because people are expecting Irish jokes to be based on 'thickness' rather than intelligence. It is the same for all the other genres – all based on unfair pictures painted over decades of manufacturing 'jokes' to have a pop at someone other than yourself.

If you scour the 'comedy' sections in bookshops, you will find numerous joke book categories – Irish, Welsh, Scottish, Celtic, etc – all containing a plethora of these 'safe' typical gags. But because of the very limited number of characteristics that have been tagged onto each target group, another technique has been adopted in order to fill these books. This is the technique of adapting 'neutral' jokes to fit one of the other genres.

"What does this technique involve?" I hear you say.

Try this:

How to write a typical ethnic joke

Simply take a joke and give the main character a name that is usually associated with the group that you want to create a joke about.

Here's a neutral joke:

> **A chap walked into a bar and went "Oof!"**
> **It was an iron bar.**

Let's make it into a Welsh joke by giving the chap a typical Welsh name. Er… let's try Dai, shall we? How does this sound?

> **Dai walked into a bar and went "Oof!"**
> **It was an iron bar.**

"Hey!" I hear you say, "It's a Welsh Joke!"

What about the Scots, then? Now, what's a typical Scottish name?

> **Jock walked into a bar and went "Oof!"**
> **It was an iron bar.**

There you are, a Scottish joke! Now, let's not forget the Irish. What's the trick again?

Think of an Irish name … er … oh, here's one :

> **Paddy walked into a bar and went "Oof!"**
> **It was an iron bar.**

Easy innit? I reckon I could write a joke about just about any race on the planet.

It's a bit of a cheat though, isn't it?

I'm not sure that there are that many original jokes going around. Lots of jokes are recycled to suit current affairs. Many so-called 'sick jokes' normally do the rounds shortly after the latest disaster or following news that some celebrity has been charged with some heinous crime against society, usually associated with sexual misdemeanours.

In the nineteen nineties, we were bombarded with jokes concerning allegations surrounding the sexual preferences of a high profile pop singer. Now, in 2005, another high profile pop singer is in the news facing similar allegations, and we are hearing the same jokes. The difference, the name has been changed!

In other words, the next time there is a major earthquake, volcanic eruption or any other type of disaster, expect a barrage of the same old jokes with their original locations changed to the current one.

Of course, jokes of this nature are going to offend someone – namely, the people who they are aimed at.

So, if this book does not contain Irish, Welsh, Scottish, Racist, sick or sex jokes, what does it contain?

In short, the jokes in here are funny

I'm not going to go into a long, laborious and pretentious literary analysis on the definition of a joke, I will simply say that these stories have made me laugh and have also gone down very well when I've passed them on to others.

I do not claim to have written any of the jokes in this book. I have merely documented the best of those I have heard in pubs, work and at social occasions.

The original sources of these are not known to me; the versions that I have heard may be far removed from their original form as tellers leave bits out or add some to fit their audience. I guess some would have been changed hundreds of times by the time they reached my ear. Some may be quite near to the original version, particularly if they had been broadcast recently on TV, radio or at a live stand-up comedy show.

I haven't seen much televised comedy as my TV seems to broadcast Soap continuously, even when there's no Soap on! I must take charge of the remote control and video recorder – that's my next New Year's Resolution. Oddly enough, I have only seen two comedians live, and, I hasten to add, none of their material is suitable for inclusion in this book!

So, all my material has come to me live from Joe Public – in other words, people who don't make a living from telling gags, but know a good joke when they hear one. Now I am passing them on to you.

All I can say now is read on and see what you think.

Before you start, I've just made up a German joke.:

'Fritz walked into a bar and went "Autsch!" It was an iron bar. '

Good one? Or did you think you might have heard it before?

The Jokes...

1

A wanted criminal was doing a bit of shopping in the local shopping centre one day, when he was spotted by an off-duty police officer. The officer phoned into the station and asked for back-up as he was going to follow the man as he went about his business.

The criminal went into the cobbler's and left a pair of shoes for repair. When he came out of the cobbler's, the uniformed officers had arrived and were waiting for him. They nabbed him straightaway and dragged him off to the cells, where he was kept in custody.

Three weeks later, he appeared in court and was given fifteen years.

On his release, he was given a sealed plastic bag, which contained all the items that he had had on him when he was arrested. He checked the bag and inside he found about eight quid in change, a bunch of keys, a comb and a small, wrinkled piece of paper. He flattened out the piece of paper and found that it was the ticket that the cobbler had given him to retrieve his shoes.

The following day, he went into the cobbler's, placed the ticket on the counter and announced that he'd come to collect his shoes. The cobbler picked up the ticket and said, "Ah, yes, pair of brown lace-ups, sir? Be ready Thursday."

2

4 February 2002 was a very bad day at the zoo. Everyone came into work that morning to a scene of utter devastation. There had been a power cut overnight and it had caused terrible problems.

John, the boss, had only just arrived, when he was met by the keeper of the tropical fish, who told him that the heaters in the tanks had gone off and all the fish had died. He now had three tons of dead fish on his hands.

Before John could say a word, the keeper of primates burst into his office and told him that the heating had gone off in the apes' compound, and, whilst most of them were OK, all the chimpanzees had frozen to death.

Then the keeper of insects burst in and announced that in a separate incident from the power cut, an elephant had slipped on a banana-skin, fallen over and landed on top of all his bee hives. He had 2.5 million squashed bees that needed to be disposed of.

John rang the council, to ask them to take the dead animals away, but they wanted too much money to do it. Then he had a brainwave. He told the keepers to shovel all the dead animals into the pig sty, and the pigs could dispose of the bodies, on the basis that "They'll eat absolutely anything." The keepers did this and left the pigs happily gobbling it all up.

On 5 February 2002, a new pig was delivered to the zoo. The new pig was introduced into the sty, and this conversation was overheard.

"How are you doing?"

"Okay. What's it like here?"

"It's not bad."

"What do you do all day?"

"Lie around in the mud, grunt a bit and generally play up to the punters."

"What's the grub like?"

"Okay. Yesterday we had fish, chimps and mushy bees."

3

It was a very, very cold day on the farm. The farmer was concerned about his stock, so he went to the field, where he saw something he'd never seen before. His entire herd of cattle had frozen solid! He touched one of his prize bulls and it fell over sideways, legs sticking out, still in the standing position.

He rang the vet. When the vet arrived, he took one look at the cattle, and said that there was only one person who could help him. He'd get on the phone right away, if the farmer was in agreement. It would cost a lot to sort the cattle out, and the vet asked the farmer if he was prepared to pay.

The farmer was keen to sort them out, whatever the cost, so the vet made a call on his mobile. About ten minutes later, a helicopter arrived and hovered over the field. A rope ladder was thrown out, and a very elderly lady climbed down it. She wandered around the field and touched each animal on the forehead with both her hands. As she did so, the animal in question seemed to come to life and start moving around the field. When she had touched every animal, she gave the vet a little wave, climbed back up the rope ladder and into the helicopter, which sped off as quickly as it had arrived.

The vet turned to the farmer and said, "Right you are, then, sorted. She'll invoice you direct."

The farmer, gobsmacked, said, "I've never seen anything like that – who is she?"

The vet replied, "Didn't you recognize her? That's Thora Hird."

4

There was a large tortoise, a medium tortoise and a small tortoise that lived together in a flat in London. The large and medium tortoises picked on the small tortoise constantly. They bullied him into doing all the housework, while they lazed around all day, watching TV and demanding that the small tortoise continually provide them with biscuits and cups of tea.

One day, they decided to go on holiday, and sent the small tortoise off to buy a map, to help them to decide where they would be going.

On his return, they spread the map out on the carpet, and decided that Porthcawl looked a nice place. That's where they would go for their holidays.

As usual, they left it to the small tortoise to pack everything, and when everything was ready, they piled the lot: tent, pots, pans, bathers, food, on top of the small tortoise, and set off empty-handed, leaving the small tortoise to struggle with everything.

As they were on foot, and had little idea about the scales on maps, it took them six months to get to Porthcawl.

As usual, as soon as they arrived, the large and medium tortoises went down to the beach and left the small one to unpack all the gear, put up the tent and get the picnic ready.

When they had had a bit of a swim, they got back to the tent and noticed that the small one had prepared a lovely picnic. Laid out on a lovely tartan blanket were sandwiches, crisps, cakes, jelly, pork pies, and cherryade.

Just as they were about to tuck in, the medium tortoise noticed there were no Scotch eggs, and asked the small tortoise where they were. The small tortoise said he'd left them on the sideboard in the flat. He assumed that the large or medium tortoise had brought them, as he couldn't carry any more.

The large and medium ones said they hadn't brought the Scotch eggs, and said they must still be on the sideboard in the flat. The large one told the small one to go back and get the Scotch eggs, as it was his fault that the picnic was ruined. The small tortoise refused, on the basis that the other two would have eaten the rest of the picnic by the time he got back.

The large and medium-sized tortoises persuaded him to go back, on the understanding that they wouldn't start till he got back, and that they'd beat him up if he didn't go.

Reluctantly, the small tortoise left to fetch the Scotch eggs. As soon as he had disappeared, the large tortoise said to the medium tortoise, "How long did it take us to get here?"

"About six months," replied the medium tortoise.

"So if it takes him six months to get back to the flat and another six months to get back here, that'll be about a year, then?" the large tortoise said.

For a year, the two tortoises sat motionless around the picnic. They hadn't spoken a word until the large one said, "Should be back anytime now."

The medium tortoise nodded in agreement. Another month went by, and they both started to look a bit concerned. After another week, the medium sized tortoise said, "I don't think he's coming back!"

The large tortoise nodded and said, "Doesn't look like it, does it? I don't know about you, but I'm starving. I'm going to have a crisp."

No sooner as he had spoken, than a little voice came from behind a nearby sand dune, saying, "You do, and I won't go!"

5

A man was rushing home from the pub. He had considered going to the toilet before he left, because he thought he may be able to make it home in time to relieve himself. He was halfway between the pub and his house when it became apparent that the situation was becoming desperate!

He decided to take a shortcut through the gardens. He had got as far as his next-door neighbour's garden, when he finally realized that he wouldn't make it, and he had to do it there, on his neighbour's lawn.

He dropped his trousers and relieved himself there and then. When he had finished, he went to his own shed, got a shovel and returned to his neighbour's lawn, to 'remove the evidence'. To his surprise, he couldn't find anything there. For ten minutes, he scoured the lawn and failed to find anything at all on the lawn for him to remove. He was very confused, but as there was nothing on the lawn, he went home and went to bed.

The next day, he was talking to his neighbour over the fence about his night in the pub – he didn't mention his little 'stop off' in his neighbour's garden, though.

His neighbour asked him, "What time did you come home?"

"About midnight," came the reply.

"And did you noticed anything strange going on?" his neighbour enquired.

"No, why?" said our hero, sheepishly.

"Because someone shat on our tortoise last night!"

6

A snail staggered into the police station, covered in blood, bruised, and with a broken shell. He told the duty sergeant that he wished to report a crime. He told the sergeant that he had been sliding down the street, minding his own business, when at least three slugs had jumped on him and beaten him up, in a totally unprovoked attack.

The duty sergeant asked the snail if he thought he'd recognize his assailants again.

The snail thought for a minute and said, "I dunno. It all happened so quick, see."

7

A man was having a round of golf, on his own, one morning. He was on the seventh tee, had lined up his shot, and planned to send the ball straight down the middle of the fairway. He swung his club for all he was worth, and sliced it very badly. The ball shot off to the right, went over the fence and bounced down the main road that ran parallel to the golf club. A motorcyclist saw the ball coming at him, and swerved to avoid it. Unfortunately, he swerved into the path of an oncoming petrol tanker, which exploded as soon as the motorcycle collided with it. Some debris from the explosion was thrown so high that it hit a passenger jet full of people going away for the summer.

The plane came down onto a railway track, killing all on board and all the passengers on two trains that were on the line at the time.

The golfer stood and watched all this, and collapsed in

tears when he realised what devastation his tee-off shot had caused.

The club professional arrived on the scene and asked the golfer why he was lying on the tee, crying so inconsolably.

The golfer related the story.

"Well, I teed off on the seventh and I sliced it. The ball caused a motorcyclist to collide with a petrol tanker. That exploded and brought down a plane, which crashed into two trains. I've killed hundreds of people. Oh, my God, whatever can I do about it?"

The professional thought for a moment and said, "Well, you obviously need to work on your grip."

Two golfers were walking from the ninth green to the tenth tee. One said to his opponent, "That's an unusual ball you have there; what is it?"

"It's called a 'Super Three', brand new technology. Marvellous, they are," came the reply.

"So, why do they call it a Super Three?" enquired his mate.

"Well, if you hit it into the rough, if it hasn't moved for five minutes, it lets out a loud 'bleep'. If you play in the winter and you hit it into a snowdrift, it glows bright red. If you hit it into water, as soon as it touches the bottom, a little airbag inside it inflates, it floats up to the top, two little paddles come out of the side and they propel the ball to the nearest bank," said the golfer proudly.

His friend was very impressed and asked, "That's great, where did you get it from?"

"Found it," came the unexpected reply.

Three men were playing a game of golf one day. The first two teed off and hit their balls straight down the middle of the fairway. The third sliced his ball, which went into the bushes and out of sight.

The first two strode up the fairway, towards their balls, and the third started to search in the bushes for his. After a few minutes, one of the golfers decided to go to help the one in the bushes to find his ball.

After a further ten minutes, the lone golfer on the fairway decided to see where his two colleagues had got to, as there was no sign of either emerging from the bushes. He hacked his way through the brambles and encountered a sight that he never expected to see on a golf course – his two friends were engaged in a frantic sex session of a homosexual nature.

When he asked them what was going on, one of the men explained.

"We found his ball about ten minutes ago. He played his second shot and sliced it again, straight into that tree. The ball bounced back off the tree, hit his head and it knocked him out! I was just trying to bring him round, that's all."

Still confused, the golfer said, "But you're only supposed to give someone the kiss of life, to bring them round!"

The other golfer, replied, "Well, I did. That's how it all started!"

10

A man drove into his golf club, early one morning, planning to have a round on his own, before the course became too crowded. When he arrived in the car park, he noticed a very attractive young lady, sitting alone in a very classy sports car.

She asked him if he was going to play, and if he was, did he mind if she joined him. The man agreed and they played a round of golf, which they both enjoyed very much.

After the game, she invited him back to her place for a coffee. He accepted the invitation and, soon after arriving at her place, they began kissing passionately.

They had such a good time that they decided to do it regularly: play a game of golf, then back to her place for a kiss and a cuddle.

After six months of the same, the man thought that he would like a bit more than the usual kissing and cuddling after the golf, and decided that, after the next game, he was going to pop the question.

So, after their next game, they went back to her place, and, when the kettle was boiling, he told his playmate that he fancied a bit more than the usual. She looked a bit sheepish and reluctantly informed him that she couldn't offer any more than the usual as she was a man in drag.

Our hero was gob smacked! He began to shake with rage, until he finally exploded with: "You bastard! We've been doing this for six months, and every week you've gone off the women's tees!"

11

One particularly obnoxious club professional put a notice on the golf club message board, offering £1000 to any player who could beat him over eighteen holes. The sign had been up for a month and he had received no challenges.

News got around the local clubs and, one day, the professional got a call from the World Blind Golf Champion, who offered to play him.

The professional declined, as he felt it would be grossly unfair, and he would feel embarrassed to take £1000 off him.

The blind golf champion felt insulted by this and upped the prize money to £5000 to the winner.

The professional couldn't resist the £5000 purse and agreed to play the blind man. He decided to set the date and asked the blind player, "When shall we play?"

The blind player replied, "It's up to you mate; which night can you make it?"

12

A guy was walking past Lords one day, and someone hit a ball out of the ground. He picked it up and put it in his trouser pocket. Two minutes later, another one flew out of the ground. He put that in his other pocket. After five minutes, he had four cricket balls jammed down his trousers. It was very uncomfortable, and he was limping down the street. A passing guy asked him why he was limping. Our hero answered, "Cricket balls."

The guy said, "I know what you mean. I've got tennis elbow."

13

Two Alsatians were in the waiting room at the vet's surgery. One of the Alsatians asked the other why he was there. He told a sad story.

"Well, the family I live with have three kids. All my life, they have taunted me and teased me. They give me toffee to eat, and laugh when my jaws get stuck together. They pull my tail. They try to ride me round the room. They put chewing gum in my ears. Yesterday, I'd had enough, and I bit one of them. Now, I'm being put down for it! It's just not fair. What are you here for?"

The other Alsatian told a very different story.

"I live with a 19-year-old model. She keeps me for protection, more than anything else. Every morning, she comes down, lets me out for a pee and then lights the fire. Yesterday, she came downstairs with a very short nightie on, and as I came in after my pee, she was bending over to light the fire. Her nightie had 'risen up' a bit and I lost control of myself."

"What happened?" asked the other Alsatian.

"Well, I'm afraid I mounted her and… er… you know… did the business."

"And you're being put down for that?" cried the other Alsatian.

"No," came the reply. "I'm having my nails clipped."

14

A squid was having a particularly bad day. He had a bad head, sore throat and a dicky tummy. As he was swimming slowly through the ocean, he was spotted by a shark, which saw the squid as a handy little snack. Just as the shark was about to attack the squid, he noticed that it was a little pale. He asked the squid if there was anything wrong with him. The squid described his symptoms to the shark, and, fearful for his own health, the shark decided not to eat the squid, in case he caught whatever he was suffering from. Instead, he offered the squid the opportunity to sit on his dorsal fin, and the shark swam near the surface, to allow the squid a bit of fresh air, to make him feel better. While they were on the surface, a huge whale swam past. The whale glanced across, saw the shark and shouted, "Oi, shark, have you been avoiding me?"

To which the shark replied, "No, whale, honest. Look, I've got the sick squid I owe you!"

15

It was the final of the Animal Football Cup. The elephants were playing the insects for the trophy, and, at half time, the elephants were 47–0 in the lead.

In the second half, the insects brought on their sub – the centipede.

The insects kicked off to start the second half, and the ball was passed to the centipede. The centipede got the ball in between his legs, and the elephants couldn't see it! The centipede zigzagged his way down the field and scored.

The elephants kicked off, and the centipede got the ball again. As before, he got the ball in between his legs, so the elephants could not see it, and he zigzagged his way down the field and scored.

There was a minute to go and the score was 47–47. The

elephants kicked off, and, once again, the centipede got the ball, ran straight down the pitch and scored. It was 47–48 to the insects! Before the elephants could restart the game, the ref blew up and the insects had won the game. The centipede had scored 48 goals on his own in the second half!

As the players were walking off the pitch, one of the elephants approached the centipede and they had a little chat.

"You had a great game, mate."

"Thanks a lot."

"I've never seen anyone score 48 goals in a match before. That was brilliant."

"Thanks, I was pleased with my performance."

"Tell me, why didn't you come on in the first half?"

"It took me the entire first half to get my boots on."

16

Two ants are hanging around the bus station one day. On the other side of the road, one spots a female centipede, walking towards the chip shop. He turns to his mate and says, "How's that for a pair of legs, pair of legs, pair of legs, pair of legs, pair of legs, pair of legs, pair of legs, pair of legs, pair of legs, pair of legs…" etc.

17

It was during one of the Papal visits to the UK when this event took place. Tired of all the fuss and palaver that followed him everywhere, the Pope decided to sneak out and have a quiet wander round the town, to see the quieter places that he was never taken to.

He was walking along an old part of the town, a cobbled road with shops on either side of it. Not used to walking on cobbles, he slipped and knocked the heel off one of his shoes. He noticed that he was quite near a cobbler's, and went into the shop to get his shoe repaired.

As soon as the Pope approached the counter and asked for the repair, the cobbler fell to his knees, bowed his head and claimed he was unworthy to do the repair as he was a Protestant. The Pope told the cobbler that all men were equal in God's eyes, and he would be honoured if the cobbler would repair his shoe.

When the repair was done, the Pope was so pleased with the job, he told the cobbler that, if he was ever in the UK again and needed any work done on his footwear, he'd always come back to him. The cobbler was over the moon with this and asked the Pope if he could put up a sign in his shop window, making it official. The Pope agreed.

After half an hour, the cobbler put a sign in his window saying, "COBBLERS TO THE POPE."

After another half an hour, the butcher, a staunch Catholic, put up a sign in his shop window, right opposite the cobbler's, saying, "BOLLOCKS TO THE ARCHBISHOP OF CANTERBURY."

A man walked up to another man in a pub and said, "VD?"

The man took great offence at this and punched him in the mouth. The first man walked off, clutching his mouth, and approached another man and said, "VD?"

Once again, he was punched in the mouth, and he walked off to someone else, and said the same thing again!

After ten minutes, our unfortunate hero had been punched by most people in the pub. He had a broken nose, two black eyes, a mouthful of broken teeth, and he was still walking around, saying "VD?" to people!

One guy, who'd watched the events with interest, took pity on him and decided he'd be more patient and try to find out what he meant, rather than beating him up, like most other people.

Sure enough, our bruised hero approached the sympathetic guy and said "VD?"

The sympathetic guy replied, "Yes."

And our hero replied, "You're on the pool table next, mate."

19

A guy walked into a pub, with a newt on his shoulder. He approached the bar and asked for, "A pint of lager for me and a thimbleful of bitter for Tiny, please."

As the landlord was pulling the pint of lager, he asked who the thimbleful of bitter was for. The guy pointed to the newt, who was still sitting on his shoulder. The landlord nodded and filled a thimble with bitter. He handed it to the newt, which started drinking it straightaway. The guy picked up his lager and he started to drink it.

The landlord, keen to make conversation, said to the guy, "So, why do you call him Tiny?"

The guy replied, "Because he's my newt."

20

Two cowboys were having a gunfight in a Wild West town. After about half an hour, one cowboy managed to shoot and kill his adversary, and the dead cowboy was lying in a pool of blood in the middle of the street. Unbeknown to him, during the gun battle, a stray bullet had ricocheted off a frying pan, hanging up outside the hardware shop, and gone across the street, embedding itself in a dog's foot, who, at the time, had been sleeping outside the saloon.

The dog got up and limped towards the cowboy who had won the gunfight. The cowboy looked at the dog. The dog looked at the cowboy, and growled.

The cowboy, tipped his hat, spat on the floor and said, "What's up with you, dawg?"

The dog replied, "Are you the guy that shot m'paw?"

21

One day, the police were called to the bank. There had been an armed robbery, and there was only one witness: a woman, who was having a cup of tea in the café opposite at the time of the robbery. She had seen it all and was in a state of shock.

She made her statement: "Well, I was having a cuppa, and I heard the screech of brakes. I looked up, and this car had stopped right outside the bank. An elephant got out, with a gun in his hand. He ran into the bank. I heard shots, and the elephant ran out with a bagful of money, got into the car, and it sped off at about 100 miles an hour."

A policeman asked her, "Was it an African elephant or an Indian elephant?"

The woman said, "Oooh, I don't know. How do you tell the difference?"

The policeman informed her that an African elephant had big ears and an Indian elephant had small ears.

The woman thought for a moment and replied, "I couldn't tell. He had a stocking over his head."

22

A bounty hunter went into a Wild West town and asked the sheriff who was the most wanted man in town. The sheriff told him the most wanted man in town was The Brown Paper-bag Kid.

The bounty hunter asked the sheriff how much was on his head. The sheriff told him that the reward was $5000, dead or alive.

The bounty hunter asked the sheriff to describe The Brown Paper-bag Kid to him.

The sheriff said, "Well, he wears a brown paper-bag shirt, brown paper-bag trousers, a brown paper-bag hat, and he goes about on a horse covered in brown paper bags."

"What's he wanted for?" the bounty hunter asked.

And the sheriff replied, "Rustling."

23

It was the 13th of last month. The vicar was walking along the High Street. He got to the corner and he heard a little voice saying, "Please don't step on me."

The vicar stopped and looked down to the floor. There, on

the pavement, was a little frog, looking up pitifully towards the vicar. The vicar looked at the frog and asked him how he could talk.

The frog told the vicar that he had been captured by a wicked witch and she had turned him into a frog. He had escaped her clutches and was looking for someone who may be able to break the spell. The vicar felt sorry for the frog and offered to help.

The frog told the vicar that the only way the spell could be broken was if someone would kiss him and let him sleep in his bed overnight.

The vicar, keen to help, picked up the frog and kissed him. Then he took him home and put him in his bed.

In the morning, when the vicar awoke, he discovered that the frog had turned into a choirboy.

And that, M'lud, is the case for the defence.

24

Two young lads in a hospital ward were discussing what they had wrong with them.

"What's wrong with you, then?"

"I'm having my appendix out. What's wrong with you?"

"I'm being circumcised."

"I've had that done."

"When?"

"When I was born. I was only six hours old when they did it."

"Painful?"

"Painful! I should say. I couldn't walk for a twelvemonth after it!"

25

One Sunday, the church organist noticed that the vicar didn't seem to be quite 'with it' as they were preparing for the early morning service. The organist asked the vicar if he was OK, and the vicar said he was concerned that his bicycle was missing, and he feared that it had been stolen.

After the service, the vicar seemed to be much happier, and the organist asked him why he had cheered up.

"It was during the service, and it came to me," the vicar began. "I was going through the Ten Commandments, and when I got to 'Thou shalt not commit adultery', I remembered where I'd left my bicycle."

26

A dog walked into a Job Centre and asked the counter clerk if they had any jobs for him. The counter clerk looked shocked, and told the dog that this was the first time he'd had such a request. He asked the dog if he could have a few hours to have a phone around, to see what he could do. The dog said that would be fine, and agreed to call back in the afternoon.

When the dog got back, the counter-clerk looked as pleased as Punch.

"I've got a job for you," he said, "£100 a week, working for the circus."

The dog looked puzzled and asked, "Why on earth would they want a plasterer?"

27

Rover was the pub dog. Every night, for fifteen years, he was in the bar, enjoying the company of the customers and snaffling up the tit-bits that they gave him. He was very popular with the kiddies in the beer garden, as well. He used to give them rides around the lawn and, in turn, they gave him crisps and nuts and made a real fuss of him.

He was certainly the most popular dog in the village – until, one day, he died.

A burial service was organised, with the vicar officiating, free of charge. There was a huge turnout and the pub held the biggest wake that had ever been seen there.

The highlight of the evening was the unveiling of a glass case, which the landlord had erected above the centre of the bar. He had cut off Rover's tail and mounted it in the case as a permanent reminder of the dog.

It was well after midnight before the landlord had got all the punters out and cleaned up the place. When he was making his weary way up the stairs, he met a strange apparition walking down the stairs to meet him. He stopped and looked and saw it was the ghostly shape of a dog!

He asked the ghost what was going on.

The dog replied, "It's me, Rover. I have come back."

The landlord was overjoyed and cried, "Brilliant! Now we can be together for ever!"

Rover replied, "I have only come back for my tail. I cannot go over to the other side, because I am incomplete. You must give me my tail back."

The landlord thought for a moment and said, "I'm sorry; I cannot retail spirits after 11pm."

28

Every night, Bob used to take his rabbit to the pub with him. Bob used to have a few pints and the rabbit loved the toasties that the landlord's wife used to make.

One night, Bob had his usual brew and the rabbit had a cheese toastie. When Bob had finished his drink, he asked the rabbit if he wanted another toastie. The rabbit nodded eagerly. Bob ordered another pint and another cheese toastie. The landlord spoke to his wife and she told him that they had no more cheese – would a ham toastie be OK?

The rabbit nodded. He ate the ham toastie, and Bob drank his pint.

Bob was ready for another, and so was the rabbit.

This time, the landlord announced that they were out of ham. Would a tuna toastie do?

The rabbit nodded. By the time Bob was halfway through his pint and the rabbit was halfway through his tuna toastie, the rabbit turned green and passed out. Bob picked him up and rushed him into the vet's surgery. The vet took one look at the rabbit and ran into the treatment room.

After four hours, the vet emerged from the room, wiping sweat from his furrowed brow. Bob, who was frantic by this time, wanted to know what the news was.

The vet said, "Well, it was touch and go for a while, but he's pulled through and I think he's going to make it. You can go in and see him, if you like."

Bob dashed in, and there was the rabbit, lying on the table. He looked a bit pale and tired, but a lot better than he had earlier.

Bob picked him up, gave him a cuddle, and with a tear in

his eye asked, "What did the vet say was wrong

The rabbit looked up at Bob, and in a very weak
uttered, "Mixin'm' Toasties."

29

A man rang Scotland Yard and told the switchboard operator
that he needed to speak to Interpol urgently. She was new
to the job and quite often put calls through to the wrong
department. She transferred the call, and a voice on the other
end said, "Good morning. Drugs Squad. How can I help?"

The caller, who was now even more desperate, explained
that he wanted Interpol and he'd been put through to Drugs
by mistake. The Drugs Squad officer put the call back to the
switchboard.

The operator transferred the call – this time, when the call
was picked up, a voice said, "Good morning, Fraud Squad,
how can I help?"

The caller was by now so irate that he was close to tears.
He explained again that he needed Interpol, and asked could
he be transferred.

The Fraud Squad officer transferred the call back to the
switchboard, and the operator transferred the call again.

This time – "Good morning, Serious Crime Squad, how
can I help?"

The caller was now in a state of utter panic, and begged
the officer to try to sort the matter out. It was vital he spoke to
Interpol immediately. The officer thought that the call seemed
so important that he left the receiver on his desk, ran down
the corridor, and asked one of the Interpol officers to come to
his room, to take the call.

                              ,t as they could to the phone – the

                        .terpol. How can I help?"
                       "Phew, thank heavens for that. Look, I
                    rthday. Can you send her a bunch of daffs
                  .d I'll call in on my way home from work
an.   1 you."

30

A chap walked into the chip shop and asked if they had
'Terminator II'.

The chip shop owner explained that the man was actually
in a chip shop, and that the video shop was next door.

The following day, the same chap walked into the chip
shop and asked for 'ET'.

The owner, once again, pointed out that the video shop
was next door.

The next day, the same chap walked in and asked for a
bag of chips. The relieved chip shop owner congratulated the
customer on finally getting the right shop, and asked him if he
wanted anything with the chips.

The chap thought for a while and said, "Er… yeah. I'll
have a 'Fish Called Wanda', please."

31

For their honeymoon, David and Rose travelled around
the USA. One day, they noticed an Indian reservation, and
decided to stop and have a look. Inside, there were lots of stalls

selling trinkets and typical Red Indian food – the usual things you'd expect to see. Right at the end of the reservation stood a tall tepee, with a sign attached to it.

Inside the tepee, the sign claimed, was Big Chief Running Dog, who knew everything in the world and also had the longest memory in the world.

David and Rose paid their dollar and went in to see the Big Chief. He was a small, wrinkled, old man, who looked at least 70 years old.

They couldn't think of anything to ask him, so David came out with a daft question, not to waste their dollar. He asked the Chief what Rose had asked to have for breakfast that morning.

Without hesitation, Big Chief grunted, "Eggs".

He was right! David and Rose left the reservation, stunned by the fact that the Chief actually knew the answer to the question.

Fifty years later, to celebrate their golden wedding anniversary, they decided to repeat their honeymoon and see if they could retrace their steps.

Sure enough, they returned to the reservation and were surprised to see that Big Chief Running Dog was still alive. They paid their dollar and went into the tepee. David had great respect for the Chief, and decided to honour him. He'd give the Chief a traditional Indian greeting. He faced the chief, raised his hand and said "How?"

Without hesitation, Big Chief grunted, "Scrambled."

32

It was late one night, and a hedgehog was waiting by the side of the M4, looking for a gap in the traffic, so that he could cross.

He had been there for about an hour, with no luck at all – the traffic was particularly heavy that night. He spotted three rabbits, bounding across the motorway and heading straight for him. They made it across safely.

The hedgehog asked the rabbits how they managed to cross so quickly. They told him that there was a knack to crossing the motorway – wait for a gap and start to cross.

"If a car comes, stop and position yourself right in the centre of the headlights. When you are right in the middle of the headlights, stay there and wait for the car to go over you, then carry on crossing. As long as you are right in the middle of the headlights, you will be safe."

The hedgehog took their advice, waited for a gap and started to cross. Sure enough, as he was half way across, a car came. The hedgehog stopped and positioned himself right between the headlights, and waited for the car to pass him.

The three rabbits watched his progress with great interest. As the car reached the hedgehog, they heard a 'SPLAT'! Something had gone wrong! They watched the vehicle as it went past them, and one of the rabbits turned to his mates and said, "I didn't know Reliant Robins were allowed on motorways!"

33

During a pub darts match, two nuns and a priest came into the bar, bought drinks and sat in the seats next to the dart board.

A player from the home side toed the oche, and threw his darts. He scored twenty with the first dart, treble twenty with the second dart, and he hit the wire with his third.

The stray dart landed on the head of one of the nuns, pierced her skull and killed her instantly.

The checker looked at the darts that were in the board, surveyed the scene of the killing and announced to the pub, "One nun dead, and eighty."

34

A man rushed into the house, one day, and announced to his wife, "Quick! Pack your bags! I've won the lottery!
His wife, overjoyed, said, "What shall I pack? Something light and summery, something warm? Where are we going?"

The man replied, "Just pack your bags, and sod off!"

35

A woman looked out of the kitchen window and saw the old mongrel from next door 'servicing' her prize pedigree poodle on the front lawn.

She ran out and beat the mongrel with a stick – he didn't stop. She screamed and shouted at the mongrel and he just carried on.

She threw buckets of freezing water over the mongrel and he carried on relentlessly.

She ran back into the house, rang the vet and asked if he could suggest a way to stop them. The vet suggested that she went back out and told the mongrel that he was wanted on the phone.

The woman asked if this would stop them.

"Well, it just stopped me!" replied the vet.

36

A rather rich lady was being chauffeured to a dinner party, when one of the tyres got a puncture. The chauffeur told the lady that he would change the wheel, and they'd be back on the road in two ticks.

After about half an hour, the lady was getting impatient, and the driver was getting frustrated, as he could not remove the hubcap. The lady asked what the problem was, and the chauffeur said that he couldn't take the old wheel off, as the hubcap was stuck fast – he could do with something to prise it off.

The lady got out of the car, opened the boot and looked in the tool-box.

"Do you want a screwdriver?" she asked.

"Yeah, may as well. I'll never get this flippin' hubcap off," came the reply.

37

A tramp went to a large mansion and asked if the lady of the house wanted any odd-jobs done. She gave the tramp a large tin of black gloss, and asked him to paint the porch.

After two hours, the tramp knocked at the door and announced that he'd done the job. She thanked him and gave him ten pounds for his trouble.

As he turned to leave, he added, "By the way, it's not a Porsche, it's a Ferrari."

38

Two female elephants went to a disco. They were sitting down, enjoying a few drinks, when a rhino, dressed in black leather trousers, a white shirt open to the waist, and a large medallion, approached their table. Both their hearts skipped a beat when they saw the glorious beast.

The rhino leaned forward and asked one of them to dance. She gratefully accepted the offer.

When they were dancing, he whispered in the elephant's ear, "What's your name, luv?"

"Nellie," she replied. "What's yours?"

"Neil," he said.

With this, the elephant collapsed!

Neil and her friend, dragged Nellie off the dance floor and sat her down in her seat. Slowly, she began to come round.

"What happened?" asked Nellie

"You were dancing and you fainted," said her friend. "You just passed out!"

"Oh I remember now," said Nellie excitedly. "You'll never

guess who I just danced with!"

"Who?" asked her friend.

"Only Rhino Neil!!" said Nellie, smugly.

39

A plumber arrived at a house, to service the boiler. The owners had forgotten he was coming and had gone out shopping. He knocked the door and the owners' parrot shouted, "Who is it?"

"It's the plumber," the plumber replied.

Thinking it was the owner, the plumber picked up his tool bag, expecting the door to be opened, so he could go in and do the job. After five minutes, he put his bag down and knocked on the door again.

"Who is it?" shouted the parrot.

"It's the plumber!" replied the plumber.

A further five minutes went by and still no-one had opened the door.

He knocked on the door again.

"Who is it?" shouted the parrot.

"It's the plumber!" replied the plumber.

This went on for an hour and a half! By this time, the plumber was so exasperated that he had a heart attack and died on the doorstep.

After five minutes, two old ladies shuffled along the pavement, and saw the body lying outside the door of the house. They looked at the body, and one turned to her friend and said, "Who is it?"

"It's the plumber!" shouted the parrot.

40

Two guys, Bob and Mike, are having a pint in the pub, when another guy comes in and stands by the bar.

"Alright, Frank?" says Bob

"Not bad," replies the guy at the bar.

"Who's he?" asks Mike.

"That's Frank," Bob says. "Surprised you don't know him. Everyone knows Frank."

"Well I don't," says Mike.

Mike was an argumentative so-and-so and challenged Bob about the fact that '*everyone* knows Frank'. He decided to put it to the test. Mike suggested that he, Bob and Frank went to a pub that none of them had ever been to.

So, they went to a town they hadn't been to before, and walked into the first pub they found. As they walked in, everyone in the pub turned round, and, as one, shouted, "Hiya, Frank!"

Mike was not the type to be beaten, and suggested they went to London, to see the Queen.

They arrived at Buckingham Palace. Frank knocked at the door. The Queen answered.

"Hello Frank!" she said. "So nice to see you; are you coming in for a cuppa?"

So, after tea and cucumber sandwiches at the palace, Bob turned to Mike and asked if he believed him now.

Mike suggested they went to see the Pope.

When they arrived at St. Peter's Square, Frank said that he'd have to go to see the Pope alone, as he was a very private person, but he would come out onto the balcony and wave to them.

Mike and Bob were waiting in the crowd for hours, when suddenly, two minute figures appeared at the balcony and started to wave at the crowd.

"There he is!" shouted Bob. "Told you, didn't I?"

The figures were so far away that Mike couldn't make out their facial features. To be sure, he decided to ask some American tourists who were nearby if he could borrow their binoculars, so he could get a good look at the people who were waving.

As he neared the Americans, one turned to his friend and said, "Say, who's that little guy in the funny hat, up there with Frank?"

41

A missionary went to visit an obscure African tribe, to preach the word of friendship to them. The chief gathered the tribe, and the missionary stood up and began.

"Brothers, it is a great pleasure for me to be here with you today."

The whole tribe, as one, shouted "Oomgawah!" in response to his opening line.

The missionary went on, "I have always had a great love of African tribes, particularly this one."

Again, the throng replied with, "Oomgawah!"

The missionary continued, "I extend a hand of friendship from my people to your people, as a token of my respect for your tribe."

Once again a loud, "Oomgawah!" followed.

In fact, throughout the missionary's hour-long speech, the tribe greeted the end of every sentence with a rapturous

"Oomgawah!"

After the speech, the chief decided to show the missionary around their village. He showed him the huts that they lived in, the cooking area, the well and the area where they grew their fruit and kept their livestock.

Just as they were entering the enclosure where the cattle were kept, the chief turned to the missionary and said, "Keep your eyes on the ground as we walk through here. You have to be careful, in case you step in any oomgawah!"

42

Two aardvarks were having a drink in the pub. The landlord came over for a chat.

"Everything to your liking?" the landlord asked.

"Fine," said the aardvarks.

"Beer OK? asked the landlord. "Not warm, is it?"

"Beer's great," said the aardvarks.

"Juke box isn't too loud, is it?" asked the landlord.

"Look," said one of the aardvarks, "everything is great, we have no complaints at all, we're having a good time."

"Well, why the long faces, then?" came the landlord's reply.

43

A guy goes into confession and says to the priest, "Father, I'm 80 years old, married, have four kids and 11 grandchildren, and, last night, I had an affair with two 18-year-old girls. I made love with both of them twice."

The priest said, "Well, my son, when was the last time you

were in confession?"

"Never, Father, I'm Jewish."

"So, then, why are you telling me?"

"I'm telling everybody."

44

A wizard was eager to try out a new spell that he'd designed, so he asked his family if they minded if he tried it out on them – they agreed.

He waved his magic wand, and, quick as a flash, his son turned into a plush armchair, his daughter turned into a super-soft, reclining chair with footrest, and his wife turned into a top class, leather three-seater settee.

He was over the moon with the spell, but this soon waned, when he found he could not reverse it – his family now seemed doomed to spend the rest of their lives as items of furniture. He dialled 999, and an ambulance turned up and took them into the hospital.

After a few hours, the wizard rang the hospital to ask how they were. The nurse put him on hold, and said she'd check them out and let him know how they were doing.

After a few minutes, she returned and told the wizard:

"They're comfortable."

45

A couple went to see a marriage guidance counsellor, claiming that their relationship had irrevocably broken down.

The wife told the counsellor, "I hate the bloke, always have done. My mother warned me about him, but I married him, anyway. Wish I'd listened to her. I hated him after the first three days of marriage, and every day I've hated him a little bit more."

The husband responded with, "This woman is the most despicable person God ever put breath into. I hate her more than words can describe. I've wasted my whole life living with this wretch. The sooner we part, the better. Perhaps I can have a decent life from now on."

The counsellor, before giving his advice, asked the couple, "Do you mind telling me how old you are?"

"I'm 99 years old," said the husband.

"I'm 95 years old," said the wife.

"And do you mind if I ask you how many years you've been married?" asked the counsellor.

"We've been married for 74 years," said the wife.

"And why have you stayed together for so long, bearing in mind how much you hate each other?" enquired the now very confused counsellor.

"Well, we thought we'd wait till the kids died," came the reply.

46

Two guys were driving a lorry through the country lanes one day, when they came across a bridge with a sign, which read "CLEARANCE: 11' 3".

They got out and measured their lorry. It was 12 feet 4 inches tall.

"What d'you reckon?" asked one, as they climbed back into the cab of the lorry.

The driver looked to his left then to his right, checked the rear view mirrors, and then selected first gear.

"No coppers about. I'm gonna chance it," he said.

47

Fred had worked on the railways for fifty years. He had started on the railways the day after he left school, and had not had a day off in all his working life. He loved the railways, and was sorry when he had to retire.

A week before his retirement, his boss asked him if he wanted anything special as a going away present, or whether he'd be happy with the usual gold watch.

As he was a complete railway enthusiast, Fred asked if he could have 100m of disused track with a buffer at each end, and a disused carriage. The boss agreed.

On his retirement, he was taken to some waste ground, and there was the carriage, on the 100m of track with a buffer at each end.

The boss asked him what he wanted it for.

"I'm going to do up the carriage and live in it," he said.

After a few months, the carriage was sparkling, was fully furnished, and had gas and electricity.

One day, his son came to the waste ground to visit. He hadn't seen his parents for over a year, and couldn't wait to see their new home.

As he approached, he could see his father standing at one end of the carriage, struggling like mad, trying to push the carriage up the tracks.

"Dad, what are you doing?" he shouted.

"Can't stop now, son; your mother is on the toilet!" came the reply.

48

Bert had worked as chief rock-maker at the local sweet factory for 25 years. Things got a bit tight, and the management decided to trim the wage bill a bit by making redundancies. Bert was one who was made redundant.

A few weeks later, Bert noticed an advertisement for a rock-maker at a different sweet factory, and sent his CV to them. The boss of the factory read Bert's CV with interest, and decided to ring his old employer, to ask what he was like. Bert's old boss couldn't speak highly enough about him. He said that Bert hadn't missed a day's work in all the years he'd known him, and there wasn't a job in the sweet industry that he couldn't do. Bert's old boss did issue one warning to his potential new boss, though, "If you ever have to make him redundant, get him to leave the premises immediately. Don't make the same mistake that we did, and give him a week's notice," he said.

"Why's that?" asked the 'new' boss.

"Because we've got three miles of rock on the shelves that we can't sell because it's got the word 'BASTARDS' written all the way through it," came the reply.

49

A man lay spread out over three seats, in the second row of a cinema. As he lay there, breathing heavily, an usher came over and said, "That's very rude of you, sir, taking up three seats. Didn't you learn any manners? Where did you come from?"

The man looked up and groaned, "The balcony!"

50

A woman had two parrots. She knew one was male and the other was female but, as they were identical, she didn't know which was which.

Then, her neighbour had a marvellous idea. He told her to put a big sheet over the cage in the night, just before she went to bed. Then, in the middle of the night, creep downstairs and listen to see if there were any 'goings on' in the cage. If there was, rip the sheet off, and whichever one was on the top would be the male.

So she did this every night. On the third night, she was listening and there was definitely 'something going on' in there. She whipped the sheet off and, sure enough, they were at it.

She opened the cage, grabbed the one on the top and put a bit of white tape around his neck, so she could tell him from the female.

Two days later, the vicar popped in for a cup of tea. The male parrot took one look at him and said, "Oh aye, caught you at it as well, did they?"

51

A woman was in bed with her lover, when she heard her husband opening the front door.

"Hurry!" she said, "stand in the corner."

She quickly rubbed baby oil all over him and then dusted him with talcum powder.

"Don't move until I tell you to," she whispered. "Just pretend you're a statue."

"What's this?" the husband inquired, as he entered the room.

"Oh, it's just a statue," she replied nonchalantly. "The Smiths bought one for their bedroom. I liked it so much, I got one for us."

No more was said about the statue, not even later that night, when they went to sleep.

Around two in the morning, the husband got out of bed, went to the kitchen, and returned a while later, with a sandwich and a glass of milk.

"Here," he said to the 'statue', "eat something. I stood like an idiot at the Smiths' for three days, and nobody offered me as much as a glass of water."

52

One day, a very grumpy customer ordered a pair of size four lace-up shoes in the shoe shop. When the assistant was about to wrap them up, the customer told him not to bother as he would wear them now. His feet were obviously much bigger than size four, and the customer really struggled to jam his feet into the shoes. When he had managed to get his feet in, he tied them as tight as he possibly could.

He stood up and staggered out of the shop, yelping with pain at every step he took.

The assistant looked at the shoes he'd left behind – the ones he had on when he came in. They were size 10! The assistant thought it was the strangest thing he'd ever seen.

About a month later, the assistant was sitting in the park, when he heard a familiar sound. It was a kind of yelping sound. He looked around and spotted the customer, staggering along, still in great pain. The assistant couldn't resist – he had to ask the customer why he had bought those shoes.

The customer told him a torrid tale.

"About two months ago," he began, "my life was a bed of roses. I was happily married, with three glorious kids. Then, one day, my wife ran off with the milkman. I was devastated! A week after that, my eldest daughter dropped out of university to live with a drug-crazed, sex maniac rock star. The following week, my son was arrested for armed robbery and given 15 years, and I found out that my youngest daughter, who is only 21, had a job as a porn actress, and has appeared in over 400 films.

If that wasn't bad enough, I lost my job and couldn't pay the mortgage. The day before I bought those shoes, I was evicted, and I am now living in a cardboard box at the back of the railway station."

"But that still doesn't explain why you bought the shoes," said the shop assistant.

"Simple," said the customer. "The only thing I've got to look forward to in life now is getting back to my cardboard box and taking these shoes off."

53

A man walked into a pub and asked for a pork pie. The landlord put the pork pie on the counter. The man paid for the pie, put it on his head and walked out of the pub!

Everyone in the pub watched in disbelief.

The next day, he did the same thing – walked in, bought a pork pie, put it on his head and walked out.

He did it every day for six months.

Everyone in the pub asked the landlord to ask the man why he did it, but the landlord didn't like to. He said he'd think of some way around it.

Next day, the man came in and asked for a pork pie. The landlord said that he didn't have any. Undeterred, the man asked for a bag of crisps. The landlord gave him the crisps, the man paid for them, put them on his head, and was just about to walk out, when the landlord, who couldn't stand it any longer, said, "Excuse me, sir, why do you do that?"

"Do what?" said the man.

"Put those crisps on your head and walk out," said the landlord.

"Because you haven't got any pork pies," came the reply.

54

A guy went to a night club and was refused entry as he wasn't wearing a tie. Desperate to get in, he ran to his car to see if there was a tie there.

He turned the car upside down – no tie! He then started to look for something – anything – that looked like a tie.

After going through the entire contents of the vehicle again, he decided that the nearest thing he had in there that remotely resembled a tie was a set of jump leads.

The guy carefully positioned the jump leads under his collar, tied a sort of a knot in them, and stuffed the grips into his inner jacket pockets, so they could not be seen.

He returned to the club, approached the doorman and asked if he could go in.

The doorman looked him up and down and said, "Well, you can come in, but don't start anything."

55

The champion at the local snooker club was itching to get onto the table to have a game and humiliate anyone who would challenge him. Nobody would!

Suddenly, the door opened and in walked a stranger. He approached the bar, bought a drink, sat down in the corner and started to read his paper.

The club champion strode across and asked him if he fancied a game.

The stranger put his paper down, looked at his watch and said, "Yeah, Ok, I've got a bit of time to spare."

The club champion let the stranger break. The stranger broke the balls and managed to pot a red off the break. He followed this with a black – the members were stunned!

In about three minutes flat, the stranger had cleared the table with a 147 break. When the last black disappeared into the pocket, the stranger put his cue back into the rack, sat down and carried on reading his paper.

The champion was furious and challenged the stranger to another game. The stranger agreed.

"I'll break this time!" growled the champion.

He broke and did not pot a red. The stranger went to the table, potted a red, and, just like before, had another 147 break – this time, even quicker than the first! He returned to his paper and started to read it.

The champion was even madder by now and decided that the stranger was just having a massive bout of beginner's luck. He decided to 'put the stranger off' by offering to play him for a large sum of money.

He strode up to the stranger and said, "I'll play you for a grand."

The stranger looked up from his paper and replied, "No way."

"Why not? demanded the champion.

"Well, I haven't seen you play yet," came the reply.

56

A man went to the Citizen's Advice Bureau and said, "I want to change my name. Do you know what I have to do?"

The advisor smiled reassuringly and replied, "Yes, I can talk you through the process. As a matter of interest, why do you want to change it?"

"Because people keep taking the Mickey out of me," the man said.

"If you don't mind me asking," said the advisor, "what is your name now?"

"Tommy Asshole," said the man sheepishly.

"Well, that is a very unfortunate name, indeed," said the advisor. "It's no wonder people ridicule you. What are you thinking of changing it to?"

"Harry Asshole," came the reply.

57

A man went to see his GP. The man was covered from head to foot in bruises, had two black eyes, a broken nose, no teeth and three broken ribs.

"What on earth happened to you?" exclaimed the doctor.

"Well," began the man, "someone knocked at the door, and, when I opened it, there was this huge beetle thing standing there. It was about six feet tall. I asked it what it wanted, and the thing just set about me and beat me up, for no reason!"

"Yes," said the doctor, "there is a very nasty bug going around at the moment."

58

Pete answered the door one day to find a very irate man at the door.

"Do you remember me? the man asked Pete.

"No," said Pete, with a puzzled look on his face.

The man went on, "Two years ago, you bought double glazing from me, and you haven't paid a penny off it yet!"

Pete, with an even more puzzled look on his face, replied, "You told me it would pay for itself in eighteen months!"

59

A man is crawling on his hands and knees across the Sahara Desert. He hasn't had a drink for three days. Suddenly, he sees a pair of sandals in front of him. He looks up to see an Arab standing there, watching him crawling around.

"Water, water," he begs.

The Arab looks at the man and says, "Wanna buy a tie? I've got striped ones, spotted ones, multi-coloured ones, tartan, checked, plain, even dickie bows."

"I don't want a tie!" cried the man, "All I want is water, Please give me some water!"

Without another word, the Arab stepped over the man and

strode off into the desert.

Our man carries on crawling, and spots an oasis far away on the horizon. He manages to get to his feet and sprints as fast as he can towards it.

As he nears the oasis, he sees it is fenced in by two smartly dressed men, guarding the entrance. He gets to the entrance, falls to his knees, right at the feet of the men, and cries, "Thank God! I'm saved! Water, water, water!"

The two guards watch him grovelling in the sand. They look at each other, and then one stoops and shouts in the man's ear, "You ain't coming in here without a tie on, matey!"

60

A guy is walking down the street when he spots a Viking leaning up against the wall near the chip shop. He looks across at the Viking; the Viking looks at the man, and they make eye contact. Immediately, the Viking shouts, "Oi, you! Come here, NOW!"

Frightened to death, the man runs across to the Viking. On his arrival, the Viking picks him up by his lapels, one handed, and lifts him up so they are nose to nose. The man's feet are a good two feet off the ground!

The Viking looks the man in the eye and growls, "Has there been any raping, pillaging, mindless violence, vandalism, robbery, heavy drinking, loud and boisterous behaviour, fighting and swearing going on around here at all this evening?"

"No, no, no," cries the man, absolutely petrified, "No, honest!"

The Viking drops him like a stone – the man ending up

in a heap at the Viking's feet. The Viking, looking puzzled, touches his bottom lip with his index finger, looks up to the skies and mutters, "Hmmm, I wonder where all the boys have gone tonight, then?"

61

The lion tamer at the circus was training his son to take over from him when he retired.

"First, you hold the whip and the stick in your left hand, and the chair in your right," he began, "then, when the lion jumps off the stool, stand your ground, Don't show him that you are scared. If he starts to come towards you, just give him a quick jab with the chair and he'll back off."

"What if he doesn't?" asked the son.

"If that doesn't stop him," continued the lion tamer, "give him a poke with the stick."

"And if that doesn't work?" the son said.

"Give the lion a lash with the whip," said the lion tamer.

"And if that doesn't work?" the son went on.

"Alternate these, in this order:" began the lion tamer, "a poke with the stick, followed by a lash with the whip, and then a jab with the chair. Keep doing these in that order until he stops."

"What if he doesn't?" asks the son.

"Walk backwards slowly, don't run, walk calmly, doing the poking, lashing and jabbing all the time," said the lion tamer.

"What if I am up against the bars, and I can't go back any further, I'm poking him, whipping him and jabbing him with the chair, and he's still coming towards me?" the son asked.

"Just bend your knees, lowering yourself down until you

can reach the floor," began the lion tamer. "Feel between your feet, pick some shit up and throw it in the lion's face. They hate that. He'll back off then."

"What if I bend down and there's no shit between my feet?" asked the son.

"There will be, my boy," said the lion tamer knowingly. "There will be."

62

One night, the local pub was taken over by hundreds of lumps of tarmac, all drinking, singing and enjoying themselves.

One went to the bar for some fags, and the landlord got chatting.

"What's going on in here tonight, then?" he asked the lump of tarmac.

"Well," began the lump of tarmac, "tonight is the lumps of tarmacs' night out. We all get together once a year for a booze-up and a sing song, and we decided to have it in here. In here tonight we have representatives from every road, by-road, lane and street in the UK.

I'm actually from the M25; that lump of tarmac by the juke box is from the A470; and that lump of tarmac, throwing darts at the moment, is from the runway at Heathrow."

As he was telling the landlord where all the lumps of tarmac were from, one lump of tarmac, who had been looking out of the window, shouted, "Look out, here he is!!!"

On hearing this, all the lumps of tarmac dropped what they were doing and hid in the toilet. The lump of tarmac at the bar told the landlord to tell the next lump of tarmac to come in through the door that he hadn't seen them. Quickly, he joined the others in the toilet.

No sooner was the toilet door shut, than the door opened and in walked a lump of tarmac. He approached the bar, all the time looking around the pub, surveying the entire area.

"Can I help you?" said the landlord.

"Any lumps of tarmac been in here tonight?" asked the lump of tarmac.

"Sorry," said the landlord, "not seen any tarmac in here for a while."

The lump of tarmac turned on his heels and walked out.

A few seconds later, the lumps of tarmac that had been hiding, started to sneak out of the toilet and get back into the swing of the evening.

The landlord spoke to one of them.

"Why were you all hiding from that lump of tarmac?" he asked.

"Oh, we don't like bothering with him," said the lump of tarmac. "He's a cycle path."

63

A man, with a cap on, went to the doctor's. The doctor asked him what the trouble was, and the man removed the cap to reveal a little green shoot that was growing out of the top of his head. He explained, "It's like this, see, Doc, about a week ago, I had this pimple on the top of my head. I didn't take any notice of it, and then, when I woke up this morning, I found that, sometime overnight, the top had come off the pimple and this little green shoot was poking out."

The doctor replied, "Well, I've never seen anything like this before. I don't know that much about plants, but I do know that if you keep the sun off it and you don't water it, it'll probably wilt and die. That's the only thing I can suggest at the moment."

"I'll try that, then," said the man. He replaced the cap, thanked the doctor and walked out of the surgery.

The next patient came in. He had a bowler hat on. He removed the bowler to reveal a flower growing out of the top of his head. He explained, "It's like this, see, Doc, about a fortnight ago, I had this pimple on the top of my head. I didn't take any notice of it, and then, when I woke up one morning, I found that sometime during that night, the top had come off the pimple and a little green shoot was poking out. I didn't take a lot of notice of it, but this morning, when I woke up, I found it had grown into a flower so I thought I'd better get it checked out."

The doctor replied, "Well, I must admit, I have seen something similar to this before, and I can only give you the same advice that I gave to the other patient. I don't know that much about plants, but I do know that if you keep the sun off it and you don't water it, it'll probably wilt and die. That's the only thing I can suggest at the moment."

"I'll try that, then," said the man. He replaced the bowler, thanked the doctor and walked out of the surgery.

The next patient came in. He had a top hat on. He removed the hat, to reveal a big bullfrog growing out of the top of his head.

"What on earth happened here?" exclaimed the doctor.

And the bullfrog said, "It's like this, see, Doc, about a month ago, I had this pimple on my arse…"

64

Three blokes were discussing what they thought had been the greatest advancements in science and technology over the last 100 years.

The first one said, "I reckon the greatest breakthrough was the kidney transplant, because if it wasn't for that, it'd be curtains for me."

The second one said, "I reckon the greatest breakthrough was the heart transplant, because if it wasn't for that, it'd be curtains for me."

The third one said, "I reckon the greatest breakthrough was the invention of the Venetian blinds, because if it wasn't for those, it'd be curtains for all of us."

65

A husband and wife were experiencing some cash flow problems, so they decided that the wife would supplement their income by selling herself at the red light area of the town. When she returned after her first stint, the husband asked, "How much did you make?"

"A hundred and twenty-nine pounds and fifty pence," she said.

"Who the hell gave you fifty pence?" the husband retorted.

"All of 'em," came the reply.

66

A man went to see his GP about a very strange-looking growth that he had on his cheek. The GP had a look at it and decided that he needed to take a closer look.

Under the microscope, the GP noticed that the growth consisted of a picturesque scene. There were some rolling hills, with the sun setting behind them. Trees swayed majestically in the warm breeze, and, standing beside a crystal clear babbling brook was a red deer stag, surveying the whole scene.

When he had viewed the whole thing, he put his microscope away and delivered his diagnosis to his patient.

"It's a beauty spot."

67

A potato went out for a few drinks and got into a fight with a bunch of carrots. He took a bit of a hiding and ended up in the local hospital.

When he awoke, he saw the doctor peering down at him. The potato asked what injuries he had sustained altogether.

The doctor told the potato that there was some good news and some bad news.

"What's the good news, Doc?" asked the potato.

"Well, we managed to save your jacket," said the doctor.

"And the bad news?" said the potato.

"You're going to be a cabbage for the rest of your life," came the reply.

68

A man walked up to the bar in a pub and asked the landlord, "A bint of pitter, please."

"Do you mean a pint of bitter?" asked the landlord.

"That's what I said!" replied the customer.

"No, you asked for a bint of pitter," said the landlord.

"I do beg your pardon," said the customer. "I get my words mixed up, sometimes."

"Funnily enough," said the landlord, "I do that as well, sometimes. I did it this morning, as a matter of fact."

"What happened?" enquired the customer.

"I got up this morning, and my missus asked me what I wanted for breakfast. All I had to say was 'bacon, egg and tomato'. And do you know what I came out with?"

"What?" asked the customer.

"I wish I'd never married you, you big, fat, useless, sour-faced cow!"

69

It was the last night of the Proms, and the whole orchestra went out for a booze-up at the end of the show. They went out for a meal first, then round the pubs, and back to someone's house.

The next morning, the piccolo player woke up on the floor in his house. He had been so drunk he hadn't been able to make it up the stairs. Extremely hung-over, he decided to make himself some coffee, to try to wake himself up a bit. He checked the cupboard, and he was out of coffee, so he decided to go to the shop to get some.

He searched the place high and low, and found that he'd lost his wallet. He knew he had it on him the night before, so he decided to go back to the other person's house, to see if he had left it there.

He couldn't remember where the house was – he had a rough idea of the area, but not of the actual house. He could remember that the house had a red front door, and that they had a golden toilet seat.

He wondered round for a few hours, knocking on red front doors, with no success. Just as he was about to give up, he spotted another red front door. He rang the bell and a woman answered, looking very hung-over and worse for wear.

"Excuse me," the piccolo player said, "was I here last night?"

"You may well have been," replied the woman, "there was a party here last night. My husband plays in the orchestra, and he had most of them around for drinks after the show last night."

"I would have been here, then," said the relieved piccolo player, "I was wondering, did I leave my wallet here?"

"We have found a wallet that we couldn't identify," she said. "Come in and see."

As he was walking into the house, the piccolo player added, "I was very lucky to find the house, I was just about to give up and go back to bed. I am feeling very rough this morning. I was so drunk last night, that the only thing I could remember about it was that you had a red front door and a golden toilet seat."

On hearing this, the woman shouted up the stairs, "Bert, I just found out who crapped in your tuba!"

70

A couple who were due to get married had two very dark secrets that they decided they weren't going to bring into the open until their wedding night.

Jackie, the bride, had terrible halitosis, and she didn't want to kiss Bob, the groom, before the wedding, in case he decided to call the wedding off.

Bob, the groom, had terribly smelly feet, and he decided that he wouldn't take him shoes off until after the wedding, in case she decided to call the wedding off.

After the wedding was finished and all the guests had left, Bob and Jackie went up to the wedding suite, to get ready to 'come clean' about their secrets.

Jackie ate lots of mints and got into bed, wondering how she was going to break the news.

Bob went into the bathroom to take off his shoes. He left his socks in a steaming heap on the floor. He went into the bedroom and lay on the bed.

"Before we start," Bob said, "I've got something to tell you."

"I've got something to tell you, as well," said Jackie.

Bob leaned over and kissed Jackie, then sat up with a start.

"I know what you're going to tell me," he exclaimed.

"What's that?" enquired Jackie.

"You've just eaten my socks!" came the reply.

71

The local town hall used to hold concerts from time to time, with local bands, guitarists, singers and so forth. Nothing very special, and they were never very well attended.

That is, until one day an agent rang Phil, the entertainments manager for the hall, to ask if one of his acts, a singer-songwriter, could play there on the following Saturday night. Phil agreed, posted some ads around the town, and added the gig to the 'What's On' section on the Town Hall's website.

Within an hour, the entire allocation of tickets was sold out!

Phone calls from all over the world were jamming the phone lines; faxes and emails were continually coming through with requests for tickets.

Within an hour, tickets were being offered on the black market for thousands, and they were being snapped up as soon as they became available.

Phil could not understand this and contacted the agent to find out why there was so much interest in the act.

The agent told him that, although the singer-songwriter was virtually unknown, he had written what was undoubtedly the greatest song that the world had ever heard. All the greatest music enthusiasts in the world were aware of the song and were desperate to hear it. The song had never been recorded, and the only chance anyone had to hear the song was to see it performed live. This is why there was so much interest.

On the Friday before the concert, people started to queue to get good seats, and the town was invaded by musicians from all over the world. There was not a vacant room in any hotel or B&B in the town. It was mayhem!

Phil decided that he was going to watch the show as well; something he rarely did.

On the big night, the singer songwriter went through his

set, and there was nothing special about the material – just average singer-songwriter stuff.

Then, with a brief introduction, he did the song.

It was a love song, and it was by far the greatest song ever written. It was so moving that grown men were reduced to tears on hearing it. No other song came anywhere near to matching the melody and the lyrics. It was tremendous.

After the gig, when all the audience had gone home, Phil was giving the singer-songwriter a hand to pack his gear away.

"That's a very beautiful song, the one you finished the show with," said Phil.

"Thanks very much," said the singer-songwriter, "it is very popular."

"Why don't you record it?" asked Phil, "You'd make millions."

"A lot of people have said the same," the singer-songwriter said. "I've taken it to all the record companies and they won't touch it."

"I can't understand it," said Phil, "it's the best song in the world. I'm sure it'll be recorded one day – it's crazy not to make a record. I will certainly buy it, when someone does decide to record it."

"Thanks very much," said the singer songwriter.

"Yes, I'll have to look out for it," said Phil. "Er, by the way, what's it called?"

"*I Love You So Much I Can't Shit,*" came the reply.

72

A man went into a library and told the librarian that he was interested in committing suicide. He asked if there was a book she could recommend.

"We have one book that can help," the librarian began. "It's called 'How to Commit Suicide'. It will be on the third shelf on the left had side of the seventh aisle."

The would-be suicide victim walked off in the direction of the seventh aisle. After ten minutes, he was back at the counter.

"It's not there!" he said.

"On, no, not again!" exclaimed the librarian. "We've had to replace that book seventeen times in the last six months! People who borrow that one *never* bring it back!"

73

One day, an elephant escaped from the zoo. Police were put on general alert and were out in force, looking for the animal. They were having no luck in finding it, until a telephone call was made to the police station. It was an elderly lady, in a state of extreme distress, and, who, obviously, had never seen an elephant before.

The call was recorded.

"Hello, it's Mrs. Jenkins here. I've just come to my allotment, and there's a great big grey thing, bigger than a cow, standing right in the middle of my cabbages. I've never seen anything like it – it's got two tails! It's pulling my cabbages out with one of them and it's … well …. You'll never guess where it's sticking them!"

74

An old hillbilly spent most of his time brewing moonshine. It was reputed to be the worst-tasting, yet strongest moonshine that had ever been made. Those who tasted it said that it was not something that you would ever want to try again. The effect, according to those few, was not unpleasant, but the effect was not worth actually drinking the stuff and suffering the appalling bouquet.

One day, a guy was sitting on the riverbank, doing a spot of fishing. He glanced up to find himself looking down the barrels of a shotgun, held by the hillbilly.

"'Ere, drink this!" said the hillbilly, throwing a bottle of moonshine into the fisherman's lap.

"Well … er …. I don't …," stammered the petrified fisherman

"Drink some, or I'll blow your head off," shouted the hillbilly.

At once, the fisherman grabbed the bottle and took six big swigs, collapsing into a heap immediately after doing so.

When he came round, he noticed the hillbilly sitting next to a tree nearby. The hillbilly noticed that fisherman had regained consciousness, and he got up and offered the gun to the fisherman.

"Why have you given me this?" asked the fisherman nervously.

"Right," began the hillbilly, "now, hold me at gunpoint, while I have some."

75

The switchboard operator at the asylum received a call from a person enquiring if there was anyone in room number 314.

"Hold on," she said, "I'll just go and check."

She returned a few minutes later and spoke to the person on the line.

"Hello caller," she said, "I've just checked and there is nobody in room 314."

"Great! I've escaped!" came the excited reply.

76

A man is fishing off a railway bridge. A passer-by notices this and decides to go over and take the Mickey out of him.

"Caught many?" he said to the 'fisherman'.

"Aye," came the reply, "you're the fourth."

77

A court case is in progress. The judge is reading the charges to the defendant.

"You are charged with beating your wife to death with a hammer."

A voice from the public gallery was heard to say
– "BASTARD!"

The judge continued, "You are further charged with beating your son to death with a hammer."

Again, the same voice filled the court with – "BASTARD!"

The judge went on, "You are further charged with beating

your daughter to death with a hammer.

Once again, the voice shouted – "BASTARD!"

The judge asked the person in the gallery to stand. A man stood up. The judge spoke to the man.

"I realise that this is a particularly nasty case, and I appreciate that you may have very strong feelings about it, but I will not allow outbursts like that in my court. Now, tell us why you have been shouting out these obscenities."

The man explained, "I've lived next door to that bastard for the last 30 years, and every time I asked him if I could borrow a hammer, he reckoned he didn't have one!"

78

A man walked into a police station with a penguin.

"Where did you get that from?" asked the desk sergeant.

"Found it walking down the road," said the man. "What shall I do with it?"

"If I were you, I'd take it to the zoo," suggested the sergeant.

Two days later, the sergeant spotted the same man, walking through town. He still had the penguin with him.

"I thought I told you to take that penguin to the zoo," the sergeant said.

"I did, yesterday," said the man. "Today, I'm taking him to the pictures."

79

Six bikers walked into a transport café. There was one other customer, a lorry driver, who was sitting alone in the corner, eating his meal.

The bikers walked over to the lorry driver and started to eat his chips. The lorry driver said and did nothing. The bikers, amused by this, ate his sausages. The lorry driver said and did nothing. One of the bikers picked up the lorry driver's egg and rubbed it into his face. They all laughed loudly. The lorry driver said and did nothing.

Then, another biker picked up the lorry driver's tea and poured it over his head. This time, seeing his chance, the lorry driver made a dash for the door. The bikers thought this was hysterical. They made their way to the counter and said to the café owner, "Not much of a man, was he?"

The owner, who had been looking out of the window, replied with, "He's not much of a lorry driver either; he's just reversed his artic over six Harleys."

80

A chap walked into a rough dockland pub. He thought he'd see what the locals were drinking, before he ordered. One really rough looking punter strode up to the bar and ordered, "A pint of rat."

The landlord grabbed a rat that was running across the top of the bar, stunned it with a bottle, stuffed it into a pint glass and filled it up with scrumpy.

The punter picked up the glass and downed it in one. Rat an' all!

"Give us another 'un," the punter growled.

The landlord grabbed a rat that was climbing up the curtain, stunned it with a bottle, stuffed it into a pint glass and filled it up with scrumpy.

The punter picked up the glass and downed it in one – rat an' all!

Our hero gulped and looked the landlord straight in the eye.

"I'll have a pint of rat, please," he said.

The landlord grabbed a rat that was rummaging around in one of the boxes of crisps, stunned it with a bottle, cut off its head with a machete, stuffed it into a pint glass and filled it up with scrumpy.

Our hero took one look at it and said, "I'm not drinking that!"

"What's wrong with it?" said the landlord threateningly.

"There's no head on it!" our hero replied.

81

It was Christmas Eve. A man answered a knock on his front door. He was surprised that there was nobody there! Then he heard a little voice say, "Oi, I'm down here."

The man looked down, to see a snail on his doorstep!

"What do you want?" asked the man.

"Can I come in?" said the snail. "It's freezing out here, and, what with it being the season of goodwill and all that…"

Before the snail could finish his sentence, the man booted the snail down to the bottom of the garden, turned and went back into the house.

It was the following Easter Monday. The man answered

a knock on his front door. He was surprised that there was nobody there! Then he heard a little voice say, "Oi, I'm down here."

The man looked down, to see a snail on his doorstep! It was the same snail.

"What do you want?" asked the man.

"What did you just do that for, then?" enquired the snail.

82

A man walked into a chemist's shop.

"Can I have some anti-perspirant please?" he asked.

"Certainly, sir," replied the chemist. "Roll-on ball, or aerosol?"

The man thought for a moment and said, "Er…. Well… actually, it's for under my arms."

83

Tom is sitting in the pub with his friend Bill. Tom is yawning all the time.

"I'm not boring you, am I?" asked Bill.

"No, I'm not getting much sleep lately," replied Tom.

"How come?" said Bill.

"Well, we've got the mother-in-law staying with us at the moment," Tom began. "She fell down and she's got both of her legs in plaster. The doctor told her not to climb the stairs to go to bed."

"That doesn't explain why you're not getting any sleep," retorted Bill.

"You ought to hear the racket she makes, shinning up the drainpipe," came the reply.

84

Mike was sitting in his terraced house, when he heard a knock at the front door. When he opened it, he saw that it was the chap from next door.

The neighbour asked, "Your front room is the same size as ours, isn't it?"

"Yes," said Mike.

"And you decorated it recently?" continued the neighbour

"Only last week," replied Mike

"Well, we're decorating ours this weekend," continued the neighbour, "and I was wondering how many rolls of wallpaper you bought for it."

"Thirteen," said Mike.

A week later, the neighbour came back.

"Remember, last week, I asked you how many rolls of wallpaper you bought for your front room?" said the neighbour.

"Yes," said Mike.

"Well, I bought thirteen, the same as you," the neighbour continued, "and I've got four rolls left over!"

"So have I," Mike said.

85

A white horse went into a pub and sidled up to the bar. The landlord asked him what he wanted.

"I'll have a whisky, please," said the white horse.

"Which whisky would you like?" asked the landlord.

"What have you got?" asked the white horse.

"Teachers, Famous Grouse, Johnny Walker… in fact, we've even got a whisky named after you," the landlord said.

"What, Eric?" asked the white horse.

86

Pete was walking down the road and was interested to see a box wagon driving down the road. He watched it for ten minutes, and noticed that the driver was continually stopping the vehicle, getting out of the cab, banging the side of the wagon, getting back in and driving a few yards, before stopping the vehicle and doing it again.

Pete soon caught up with the vehicle and, when the driver got out to bang the side of it again, Pete asked him what he was doing.

"Well, I've got a load of budgerigars on," he began. "I have fifteen tons of them on board, and I can only officially carry ten tons, so I've got to keep them airborne."

87

Fred is just about to go into the pub, when a nun approaches him.

"Do not enter that vile place!" she shouted.

"What?" retorted Fred.

"Don't go in there," she continued, "You may be tempted to partake of the evil booze."

"I bet you've never even tasted booze, luv," replied Fred. "Why don't you come in and have one with me; perhaps you'll like it."

"I cannot enter such a building," the nun said.

"Well, why don't I bring one out for you?" said Fred. "You can't knock it until you try it, I always say."

"Alright," said the nun, "but bring it out in a china cup so that nobody can see what I'm drinking."

Fred walked up to the bar and ordered a pint, and a gin in a china cup.

The landlord raised one eyebrow and said, "That blinkin' nun is still out there, is she?"

88

Daddy bear came downstairs for his breakfast, one morning, looked into his empty bowl and said, "Someone's been eating my porridge!"

Baby bear came downstairs for his breakfast, soon after, looked into his empty bowl and said, "Someone's been eating my porridge!"

Mummy bear came in from the kitchen, looked at both of them, tutted, and said, "I haven't made it yet."

89

A man was in court for stealing a tin of peaches. He was found guilty, and the judge told him that he would give him one year in prison for every peach that was in the tin.

The prosecution barrister opened the tin and found that

the tin contained seven peaches.

"I therefore sentence you to seven years," said the judge. "Do you have anything to say, before they take you down?"

"I'm glad I put back the tin of peas," the accused replied.

90

A rabbit walked into a grocer's shop, banged his paws ten times on the counter and said, "A pound of carrots please."

The grocer replied, "Certainly, but please do not bang the counter with your paws if you come into this shop again."

The next day, the rabbit walked into the grocer's shop, banged his paws ten times on the counter, and said, "A pound of carrots, please."

The grocer replied, "Certainly, but please do not bang the counter with your paws if you come into this shop again. I don't want to have to tell you again!"

The next day, the rabbit walked into the grocer's shop, banged his paws ten times on the counter and said, "A pound of carrots, please."

This time the grocer said, "Certainly. By the way, the last few times you've come into this shop, I've asked you not to bang the counter. This time I'm *telling* you. If you bang the counter with your paws again, I'll nail them to the counter with six inch nails."

The next day, the rabbit walked into the shop and said to the grocer sheepishly, "Got any six inch nails?"

"No!" said the grocer with a smile.

The rabbit banged his paws ten times on the counter and said, "A pound of carrots then, please!"

Jack was leaning up against the bar having a quiet pint, when he heard a voice saying, "What a lovely tie, really goes with your shirt. And those shoes, I bet they cost a few bob, real quality, those. Still, it's only to be expected from a smart guy like you."

Jack looked around, to see who had made the comments, and there was nobody about! He was a bit unnerved by this, and he moved away from the bar and stood by the juke box.

He heard another voice.

"Oi, did you pick your nose, when you were a kid? Eh? Well, if you did, you could have picked a better one than that! Who the hell cut your hair? I'd sue whoever it was, if I were you!"

Jack looked round, to see who had made the comments, and, once again, there was nobody there! He quickly moved back to the bar. Suddenly, the landlord appeared, and noticed the strained look on Jack's face.

"Everything alright?" asked the landlord.

"Not really," said Jack. "When I was standing here earlier, someone made some really nice comments about me. Then, I stood over there by the juke box, and I was really insulted. The trouble is, I don't know who made them. I'm the only one in here."

"Oh," said the landlord, nodding knowingly, "don't worry about that; I know where those comments came from."

"Where?" insisted Jack

"Well," began the landlord, "the peanuts on the bar are complimentary, and the juke box is out of order."

Two men, Mike and Bill, were having an argument. Mike reckoned he was the biggest liar in the world. Bill disagreed with him, claiming that he was the biggest liar in the world.

As they were getting nowhere, Bill decided that they would sort the matter out once and for all.

"Right," said Bill, "what was your greatest lie of all time, Mike?"

"Last week, I tight-rope walked over Niagara falls, blindfolded!" said Mike proudly.

"I know," replied Bill smugly, "I saw you do it."

Tom was chatting up a girl in the pub. He was doing well; she was pleasant to him. They were having a good laugh. He had bought her about ten drinks, and thought he was in with a good chance.

When she went to the toilet, the landlord leaned over and had a word on Tom's ear.

"You're wasting your time there, mate," he said, "she's a lesbian."

Tom shrugged his shoulders and ordered another drink for her.

She returned from the toilet and sat down. Tom leaned forwards, looked her in the eye and asked, "So, what part of Lesbia are you from then, luv?"

94

Alan was out on the prowl in the red light district. He looked at all the really attractive girls, with the usual gear on: short skirts, stockings, low cut tops, and he didn't seem interested. He spotted a really rough looking girl. She had long, scraggy, ginger hair, she was thinner than a rake, had big bags under her eyes, a wrinkly face and she was about 60 years old.

"How much do you charge?" he asked.

"Tenner," said the woman.

Alan agreed, and they went back to his house. It was pouring with rain. By the time they arrived, she looked even more bedraggled than before. Her ginger hair was hanging down like rat's tails, and her black eye make-up had run all down her face.

"What do you want me to do?" she said, when they got inside.

"Just sit there for a minute," said Alan. "Here's your money," he said, thrusting a £10 note into her hand.

She sat in the chair and waited, while Alan left the room. Two minutes later, he returned with a red setter. He sat in the chair opposite the woman and called the red setter over to him. When the dog was sitting quietly, he pointed at the girl and spoke to the dog, saying, "Now then, that's what you'll end up looking like if you don't eat your food."

95

Jim had got a job as an actor. He was very proud. He didn't have a big part but it was a very important one. His only appearance came right at the end of the play, and he had to speak the line, "IT IS!"

Although it was his first role, he was over the moon – his line was the last line to be spoken in the whole play! He was determined to make a good job of it.

For six months, he practiced the line constantly. He'd be in the queue to pay at the supermarket, and, suddenly, he'd hold out his hand, look to the skies and shout, "IT IS!"

He'd do it when he was washing up, when he was in the pub, at the races, in church, everywhere! He had it off to a tee.

When the big opening night came, it came to the end of the play, and the producer whispered to Jim to go out and do his stuff.

Jim strode out onto the stage, looked at the audience, raised his hand, threw back his head, looked to the skies and shouted, "IS IT?"

After the play, the producer went mad! He told him that he had ruined the play and that he was sacked.

A crestfallen Jim said, "But you can't sack me!"

"Why ever not?" screamed the producer.

"Because I know my lines backwards!" said Jim.

96

It was a round-the-world cruise. The ship's magician was giving a show at the evening cabaret. It was not going all that well, really. When the magician pulled a rabbit out of the hat, the ship's parrot shouted, "There's a false bottom in the table, and a hole in the hat; that's how the rabbit gets in there."

Then, when the magician made a playing card disappear, the parrot shouted, "It's up his sleeve!"

When the magician was sawing his wife in half, the parrot

shouted, "There's two women in that box!"

Half way through the act, the ship struck an iceberg, and sank in about three minutes flat.

The magician was floundering through the water, hanging on to a piece of wood, when the parrot swooped down and landed on the wood, next to the magician.

He looked the magician in the eye and said, "Okay, you've got me on this one. What have you done with the ship?"

Ted got a job as a security guard at the local building site. A lot of stuff had been pinched from the site, and the foreman told Ted to check everybody leaving the site, and make sure that they weren't taking anything from there that they shouldn't be taking.

Ted counted all the men coming into work in the morning, and counted them going out in the night. There was one short! He scouted round the site and saw one guy trying to sneak out. He was looking very suspicious and was pushing a wheelbarrow with a piece of tarpaulin over it.

"Got you!" said Ted. "Nicking stuff, are you?"

"No," replied the guy.

"What have you got under the tarpaulin?" said Ted.

"Nothing," came the reply.

Ted whipped off the tarpaulin to reveal – nothing! The wheelbarrow was empty.

The next night, exactly the same thing happened. In fact, the same thing happened for six months, and every time Ted removed the tarpaulin from the wheelbarrow, there was never anything under it.

One day, Ted was sacked, because the foreman was losing thousands of pounds in replacing stolen items, and Ted had not caught one person pilfering from the site.

Twenty years later, Ted was in a pub and noticed someone he recognized. It was the 'wheelbarrow man'.

Ted went over and spoke to him.

"I don't know if you remember me," began Ted, "but I was the security guard on the building site where you used to work."

"I remember you," said the wheelbarrow man.

"Look," said Ted, "It doesn't matter now, but I knew you were nicking stuff from that site. I never caught you, but for my own peace of mind, what were you nicking?"

"Wheelbarrows," came the reply.

98

Rob was in town, looking to buy a birthday present for his wife. He walked past a shop window and glanced at the display. There was nothing in the window at all, apart from a very large and expensive-looking pearl necklace. That'll do, he thought, and walked into the shop.

A smartly dressed man approached him.

"How much is the necklace?" enquired Rob

"Not for sale," said the man, "We don't sell jewellery."

"What do you sell, then?" asked Rob, confused by now.

"Nothing," said the man.

"What do you do, then?" asked an even more confused Rob.

"We are a specialist vets," said the man, "and all we do is castrate cats and dogs."

"Then why have you got a pearl necklace in your window?" Rob asked.

"And what do you suggest we put in the window, sir?" replied the man.

99

Kev walked up to the foreman at the building site and asked him if there were any vacancies for a handyman. The foreman looked interested and took Kev into the cabin for an interview.

"So you're a handyman, then?" said the foreman.

"That's right," said Kev.

"Great," said the foreman, "start work in the morning with the brickies."

"Oh, I've never done any bricklaying," said Kev.

"Plastering?" said the foreman.

"Er... no," said Kev.

"Carpentry?" asked the foreman.

"Nope," said Kev.

"So, you've never done any bricklaying, carpentry, or plastering," began the foreman. "What about plumbing, roofing, tiling, painting, electrics, labouring? Done any of those?"

"None of them," Rob said.

"So, why do you think you're a handyman, then?" asked the foreman.

"I only live over the road," replied Kev.

100

A stranger walked into the pub one night, and bragged that he could drink absolutely anything. Furthermore, he challenged everyone in the pub to bet him £10 to drink something of their choice, and he would take up the bet.

After a few hours of drinking just about every strange concoction that the locals could make up, the stranger had managed to drink them all, and had made hundreds of pounds. He even drank the contents of the slops bucket!

Seeing the slops bucket empty, one man approached the stranger and bet him £100 that he couldn't drink the slops bucket, full of raw eggs, down in one.

The stranger thought for a moment, and, without saying a word, left the pub. A huge cheer went round the pub, and the locals hailed the challenger as the man who had beaten the stranger.

Five minutes later, the stranger was back.

"I'll do it!" he shouted.

The pub was silent as they watched the landlord cracking eggs into the bucket.

When it was full, the stranger picked up the bucket, put it to his lips and downed it in one. Beaten, the challenger congratulated the stranger on his feat and paid the £100 to him.

"That was tremendous," he said to the stranger. "You deserved the £100. But tell me, where did you go, when you left the pub earlier?"

"Down the 'Rose and Crown', to try it out," replied the stranger.

More Welsh laughs from David Jandrell...

Welsh Valleys Humour

David Jandrell

A tongue-in-cheek guide to the curious ways in which Valleys inhabitants use English, together with anecdotes, jokes, stories depicting Valleys life and malapropisms from real-life Valleys situations!

£3.95
ISBN 0 86243 736 9